Contents

Pages

The Importance of Being a Dad

- Being a dad is a big responsibility and one that lasts a lifetime.

- It is the most rewarding job that you will ever do, but probably the most demanding one too.

  And it's probably one that you feel least prepared for!

- You may or may not have planned to become a dad. You might feel:

EXCITED

ANXIOUS

???????

AFRAID

WORRIED

HAPPY

EMOTIONAL

PROUD

All these emotions are completely normal!
It's a big change in your life!

The Importance of Being a Dad

The most important thing is to get involved now, right from the start.

- Support your partner throughout the pregnancy, even if it means going out at midnight to buy rice pudding!

- Go along to antenatal appointments if possible.

- Choose to quit smoking and drinking to support your partner - it will be much healthier for all of you.

> The baby wants sardines and rice pudding not me!

- Attend parenting classes together. This is also a great way to meet other dads-to-be and swap notes!

- Be prepared for your partner's mood swings - it's a very emotional time for her too.

- Budget and plan for your baby's arrival. For advice on what you are entitled to, contact your local Citizens Advice Bureau see page 27.

LIST
NAPPIES

The Arrival of a New Baby

I think the baby is coming!

Be prepared

Discuss a birth plan with your partner - before it's too late!

- Plan how you will get to the hospital.

- Pack a hospital bag.

- Arrange who will look after other children.

- Have the number of the hospital ready to call.

- Don't panic!

Be there at the birth

Don't worry about what to do, just support your partner.

- Hold hands.

- Be patient!

- Help with breathing exercises.

- Have your phone ready to share the good news.

Be there to welcome your baby into the world

The Arrival of a New Baby

Taking baby home

- Don't worry you and your partner will soon learn what to do.

- Support each other and talk.

- Don't be afraid to ask your midwife, health visitor or doctor for advice.

- Register your baby's birth at the local registry office and the doctors.

What about you?

- Things will change - you're a family now, not just a couple.

- The first few months of parenting can strain your relationship.

- Work together as a team, share things and don't forget to take care of each other as well as baby.

- Don't forget contraception when the time is right.

My six-week check up was fine and baby's doing great!

Staying Safe

- The best place for baby to sleep for the first six months is in a cot in your room.

- Make sure that everything is close by when changing your baby.

- Never leave a baby alone on a raised surface.

- Never leave a baby or young child alone in the bath.

- Always use safety straps in baby seats, highchairs, buggies and car seats.

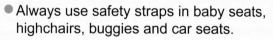

- Don't forget the importance of a car seat for every journey. Make sure that it is the correct size for your child and correctly fitted.

Staying Safe

Reduce the risks at home!

Fit safety gates

Fit a fireguard

Don't leave cables dangling

Make children aware of dangers
and how to keep safe.
It's never too early to start.
Explain why - don't just say NO!

Store away all cleaning materials

Lock up medicines

Keep hot drinks out of reach

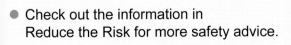

● Check out the information in
  Reduce the Risk for more safety advice.

Being Healthy

You will need to look after yourself if you are going to be able to look after your kids well.

Set a good example:

● Eat a healthy diet.

● Get regular exercise.

● Don't drink to excess.

● Say **NO** to smoking or drugs.

Being Healthy

The NHS provides health checks and vaccinations free of charge for all children.

- Speak to your health visitor or GP to make sure that you take advantage of all that is offered for the well-being of your children.

- Register your child with a dentist as soon as the first tooth appears.

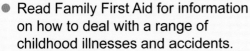

- Read Family First Aid for information on how to deal with a range of childhood illnesses and accidents.

- If you are worried or concerned you should always ring your GP or **NHS Direct on 0845 4647** for help and advice.

Healthy Eating

Breast is best for the first 6 months

But don't feel left out!
You can still be involved by winding your baby after the feed, or your partner can express breast milk if you want to feed your baby.

If you are using formula milk always follow the instructions carefully.

Don't forget that all bottles need to be sterilized for the first 12 months.

BUUURP!

Introduce your baby to solid foods at about 6 months

Start by giving a few teaspoons of mashed vegetables, fruit or baby rice mixed with breast milk or formula milk.

Don't worry about the mess!

Gradually introduce different tastes and textures.

A plastic cover under the highchair is a good idea!

Healthy Eating

A healthy diet is important for all the family.

mmm I think I'll eat all my yummy brocolli!!

Sit down at the table and eat together as often as possible.

Children love to copy - so set a good example!

Keeping Active

Keeping active is important for all the family and great to enjoy together.

● Walking in the park

● Splashing in puddles

● Kicking leaves

● Pushing swings

Keeping Active

● Riding bikes

● Playing ball

● Enjoying team games

Get involved - helping to run a junior sports team can be great fun for you as well as your child!

Sporting activities and team games are a valuable part of your child's learning.

Early Learning

It's never too early to start **talking** and **listening** to your baby.

- Holding your baby

- Singing rhymes

- Playing together

- Sharing books

- Doing everyday activities

All these things are important learning activities and great fun for you and your child.

Early Learning

- Visit places and try new activities with your children.

- Enjoy doing everyday activities together such as making a meal, cleaning up or washing the car.

- Let your children enjoy getting messy!

- Having a go is the best way to master new skills.

- Visit your child's nursery or school for parent's meetings and other events.

- Talk to your children about their day.

- Help with homework.

Praise your children's achievements

Rules and Boundaries

Well done for tidying your bricks away!

I can't wait! It's nearly story time.

- The best way to encourage your children to behave well is to praise good behaviour.

Wow, you're making a lovely job of brushing your teeth!

- Routines and boundaries need to be agreed and will make life easier for all the family.

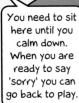

You need to sit here until you calm down. When you are ready to say 'sorry' you can go back to play.

BE CONSISTENT!

- Children need to know what is expected.

I promise I'll come and read you a story as soon as I've put your sister to bed.

- Don't make threats or promises that you can't follow through.

Rules and Boundaries

● Be calm - try not to shout and scream at your children.

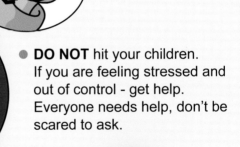

● **DO NOT** hit your children. If you are feeling stressed and out of control - get help. Everyone needs help, don't be scared to ask.

● Positive Parenting will give you more information on how best to manage your children's behaviour in different situations.

Dads who are the Main Carer

- Make sure that you get out and about with your children - don't be intimidated by other parents, especially mums!

- Dads have loads of unique skills to offer children's centre groups, nurseries and schools - you will be in demand once people get to know you.

- Remember, dads have the same rights as mums.

Dads who are the Main Carer

- Don't try and do everything single-handed, accept help and support from family and friends. Mums need this too!

GOAL!!

- Make time for yourself.

- Don't be too hard on yourself - you don't have to be perfect.

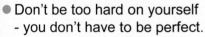

- Enjoy being a dad, but when you do get some time to yourself relax and enjoy that too!

Dads who don't Live with their Children

Explain why you can't live together - children will cope with a separation much better if they know what's going on.

- Be honest.

We just think it will be better for everyone if mummy and daddy live apart.

- Don't make promises that you can't keep.

You need to know that your mum and I still love you very much!

I love you too dad.

- Make sure that your children understand that it's not their fault.

- Keep in touch.

Although it may be difficult for you at first, a good relationship with your child's mum will make life much better for everyone, especially your child.

Dads who don't Live with their Children

When you do see your children:

- Establish normal routines.

> YEY!! HELLO NANNA!

- Remember that you don't need a special outing every time.

- Enjoy playing and doing everyday activities together.

> Well I know mum said you couldn't have it, so I thought that I would buy it for you instead!

- Don't try to buy your children's affections.

Enjoy being with your children and take an interest in everything that they do

Enjoy your Children's Company

Kids love to bake and eat the results!

Gardening can be great fun.

Bath-time is splash time!

Reading a bedtime story is a relaxing way to end the day.

Enjoy your Children's Company

How many blue cars can you count?

- Look out for things when you are travelling.

- Enjoy your local park.

- Go Swimming.

- Find out about special events in your area from your children's centre, library or local paper.

- Try to spend at least 15 minutes, per child, per day, special time.

HAVE FUN TOGETHER!

Support

Every Child Matters

The Government's aim is for every child to have the support needed to:

- be healthy
- stay safe
- enjoy and achieve
- make a positive contribution
- achieve economic well-being

Supporting you as a parent is an essential part of achieving this aim.
We all need to feel loved and cared for - children **and** adults.

Family & Friends

Family, friends and neighbours can be a great source of informal advice,
providing a listening ear, hands on practical help and of course babysittin

Your health visitor, school nurse or doctor will always be there to provide
professional advice and support and can also introduce you to other
support networks in your area.

**Ask for help if you need it, you owe it to your child.
Don't struggle alone!**

Add your local Children's Centre details here